HURRICANES

DISASTERS

Merrilee Hooker

The Rourke Corporation, Inc.
Vero Beach, Florida 32964

Edited by Sandra A. Robinson

PHOTO CREDITS
© Helen Longest-Slaughter: title page, p. 21; © Lynn M. Stone: p. 8;
© Tamara Ann Photography: p. 12, 15; © Steve Bentsen: p. 13;
© Robert Perron: p. 18; courtesy NASA: cover, p. 4, 7, 10, 17

Library of Congress Cataloging-in-Publication Data

Hooker, Merrilee, 1955-
    Hurricanes / by Merrilee Hooker.
      p. cm. — (Discovery library of disasters)
    Includes index.
    Summary: An introduction to hurricanes, describing their causes
and destructive force, how they are predicted and named, and
how to protect people from these terrible storms.
    ISBN 0-86593-243-3
    1. Hurricanes—Juvenile literature. [1. Hurricanes.] I. Title.
II. Series.
QC994.2.H66 1993
551.55'2—dc20
                                      92-42920
                                        CIP
                                        AC

Printed in the USA

TABLE OF CONTENTS

HURRICANES

A hurricane is a large, extremely powerful windstorm. It moves in a spiral shape and produces thunder, lightning and heavy rains.

When viewed from above, a hurricane is quite round. It can have a diameter of 450 miles. A hurricane can travel hundreds of miles before dying out.

A storm must have winds blowing at least 75 miles per hour to be a hurricane. Many hurricanes carry winds up to 200 miles per hour.

Hurricanes that strike land can create major **disasters.** These are events that cause terrible losses of life and property.

Hurricane Elena, photographed from above by the NASA spacecraft Discovery

HOW A HURRICANE BEGINS

A hurricane begins when a warm, wet mass of air over the sea begins to rise quickly. The combined actions of air, water and heat may then produce a huge, spinning system of clouds, rain and wind— a hurricane. The center, or **eye,** of a hurricane is calm. It is the hole in a doughnut of wind.

A hurricane usually lasts nine to 12 days. It forms and builds strength over warm sea water. It loses energy as it moves over cooler sea water or land.

The eye of a hurricane, surrounded by dense clouds and mighty winds

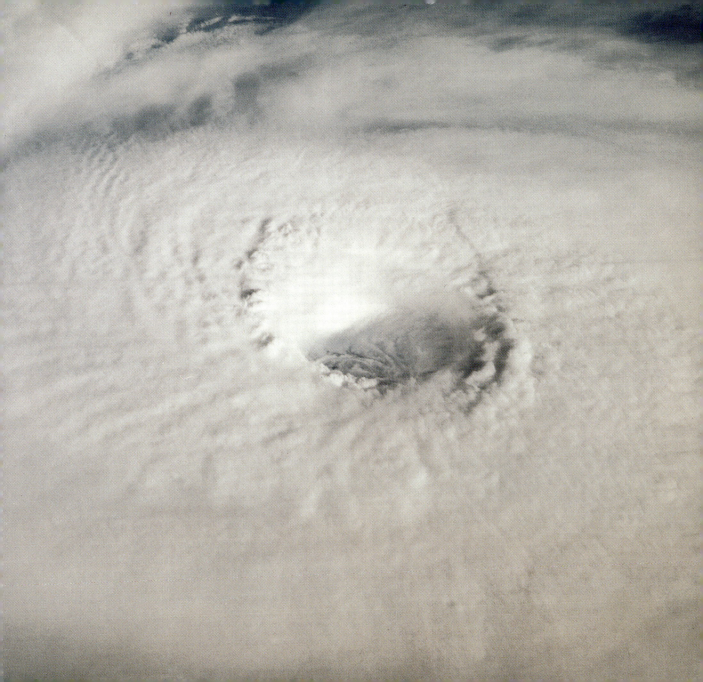

HOW HURRICANES WORK

When a hurricane and its winds strike, they tear roofs off homes, and blow trees and electrical wires down. High waves, stirred up by the wind, surge onto beaches. Sea water floods coastal homes and roads.

Rain normally falls downward. However, hurricane winds may be so powerful that they blow the rain sideways.

Flooding causes much of a hurricane's damage. As many as nine out of every 10 deaths caused by hurricanes are due to high water.

A hurricane signals its charge ashore with rising waves and wind

WHEN AND WHERE HURRICANES STRIKE

Hurricanes form over warm ocean water. They usually develop during the late summer.

No two hurricanes follow the same path, or track. Hurricanes do follow general paths in the areas where they occur.

Hurricanes that strike the mainland of the United States form in the South Atlantic Ocean or Caribbean Sea. From there they move in a northerly direction. They may strike Caribbean islands, the states along the Gulf of Mexico, and the coastal Atlantic states.

In the Indian Ocean, hurricanelike storms are called tropical cyclones.

*A hurricane developing in the Pacific
Ocean, as seen from space*

The American Red Cross and other service organizations help needy people after a hurricane strikes

*Hurricane Gilbert's high wind and water buried this car
in the sands of Padre Island, Texas*

HURRICANE DISASTERS

In this century, several deadly hurricanes have blasted Hawaii and the eastern coasts of the U.S. mainland . The worst disaster was in Galveston, Texas, on the Gulf of Mexico. A hurricane killed 6,000 people there in 1900.

The vicious Labor Day Hurricane of 1935 ripped through the Florida Keys, and some 500 people died.

In August, 1992, Hurricane Andrew leveled much of Homestead, Florida. Thousands in the Miami-Homestead area were left homeless. Damage was counted in the billions of dollars.

Much of Homestead, Florida, was smashed by the winds of Hurricane Andrew in 1992

STUDYING HURRICANES

Meteorologists are scientists who study weather. They use airplanes, satellites and other scientific instruments to keep track of a hurricane's location, speed and direction. The meteorologists measure the storm's wind speed with an **anemometer.**

Meteorologists follow a hurricane's trail carefully and try to predict where the storm will go. However, trying to know where a hurricane will strike next is much like trying to figure out which way a snake will twist next.

A NASA rocket with a weather satellite blasts from its launch

HURRICANE NAMES

During World War II (1941-1945), military weathermen began to name hurricanes after their wives and girlfriends.

The practice of naming hurricanes for women continued for many years. Today, however, the National Weather Service makes an alphabetical list of female and male names for hurricanes.

Many ocean storms that could become hurricanes fizzle, but once a true hurricane develops, a name is given to it.

Every five years a new list is made, and names of major hurricanes are not used again.

Some of the most feared hurricanes of recent years were named Donna, Camille and Andrew.

A hurricane named Hugo punched a new ocean channel through this island in South Carolina

HURRICANE WARNINGS

The National Weather Service tells people where hurricanes are over the ocean, and where they will probably come ashore. Radio and television stations broadcast information gathered by the National Weather Service.

A **hurricane watch** means people should prepare for the possibility of a hurricane occurring within two days. A **hurricane warning** means a hurricane will probably strike in the next 12 hours.

Thanks to hurricane warnings, tourists in Everglades National Park had left for safety when Hurricane Andrew hit

PROTECTING PEOPLE FROM HURRICANES

People who live along the coasts of the Gulf of Mexico, the Caribbean Sea and the Atlantic Ocean should always know what to do when a hurricane develops. If they have time, people cover their windows with boards. Often, people need to **evacuate,** or leave, the area. Hundreds of construction workers died in the 1935 Labor Day Hurricane because they were not evacuated from the Florida Keys on schedule.

Keeping a radio on is important. Weather reports tell people where to go for safety and when it is safe to return to their homes.

Glossary

anemometer (an eh MOM eh ter) — an instrument that measures wind speed

disaster (diz AS ter) — an event that causes a great loss of property and/or lives

evacuate (ee VAK u ate) — to leave a threatened area

eye (I) — the calm center of a hurricane

hurricane warning (HER uh kane WORN ing) — a report that a hurricane is likely to strike within 12 hours

hurricane watch (HER uh kane WAWTSH) — a report that people should prepare for a hurricane to occur within two days

meteorologist (meet ee er AHL uh jihst) — a scientist who studies the weather

INDEX